Are you tired (anxious at net

Don't worry. You're not alone.

Many people aren't confident when it comes to networking. They either haven't been taught how to do it or they are approaching it with an "old school" mentality. In this e-book, we will guide you through all you need to know to make authentic connections that will lead you to a future filled with opportunities.

Networking is just a fancy word for connecting with people. It's the act of making your network bigger by connecting with people and building relationships with them. Events are great opportunities to begin a new connection and start a conversation with someone you don't already know.

Networking is important because every opportunity you get in life comes from **people**. The job you want, the next client you're pursuing, the cause of the charity you volunteer for—all of them come from the relationships you have with other people. So the bigger your network is, the more opportunities you open up for yourself.

Other benefits of learning how to network include:
- Knowing how to effectively communicate with other people
- Navigating through difficult conversations
- Learning from people you might have never talked to before
- Building self-confidence and self-esteem
- Becoming a better presenter, negotiator and influencer
- Making your current relationships stronger and more meaningful

Now many people mistakenly believe that networking is collecting lots of business cards and creating long email lists of people they spoke to for five seconds. This is NOT networking. Let's repeat that again because it's so important to understand this—**collecting contacts is not networking**! Effective networking is based on relationships and trust. People won't give you opportunities because they saw you for five seconds at an event.

They'll give you opportunities because they got to know you at an event **and beyond**.

Think about it this way...imagine someone came up to you at a networking event, quickly told you what they did, hastily tried to exchange cards with you and took off. Now imagine another person, who is in the exact same business as the first person you met, came up to you, asked you what you did, shared what they did, bonded with you over a common interest you discovered, and then naturally exchanged business cards with you.

Who would you remember to call when you need their services?
Who would you look to hire when you had to fill a position?

The answer is pretty obvious. We want to share opportunities with people we trust, 'like' and have a relationship with. That's what networking is about—always and forever.

We have designed this book in a way that teaches you various tactics to use throughout the *five stages* of a live event networking opportunity, which include:

Stage 1: Preparing for Networking
Stage 2: Starting a Conversation
Stage 3: Carrying a Conversation
Stage 4: Ending a Conversation
Stage 5: The Follow-up

Take some time to learn them and then more importantly go out and apply them. As we like to say, **practice makes permanent**. As you grow your confidence in using these tools and tactics, we know you will start to see incredible results.

So have fun and enjoy the process!

Bobby and Ryan

Networking @ Live Events

Stage 1: Preparing for Networking

BUILD A PROPER MINDSET

Your journey toward being a powerful networker begins well before you actually walk into the room.

To make effective and lasting connections, you need to approach every opportunity with the right *mindset*. This means the internal dialogue that's going on in your head must be programmed to help you rather than hurt you.

The best way to do this is to ask yourself the following questions before attending an event:
1) Why am I going? What are my objectives?
2) Why are others going? What are their objectives?
3) Why do I want to meet others?
4) Why do others want to meet me?

These may seem like obvious questions, but you'll be amazed by how important they are for clarity. You need to think about them consciously. It's amazing how many events people go to where they are scared to talk to others because they think others don't want to meet them. Beliefs from our past can creep up on us all and negatively affect us if we don't purposefully set ourselves up with the right mindset.

SET GOALS FOR THE EVENT

One thing we love to say is, *"You can't accomplish what you don't see as an accomplishment."*

Every attempt to network should have a goal, even if that goal is simply to talk to one person. Goals give us a way to measure our success and experience a feeling of progress. They can be modest at first, but they will become bigger as you build more confidence.

The best way to set goals is to ask yourself the following questions for each goal you set:

1) What do I want to accomplish?

- Make this tangible and specific so you know when you actually accomplish it, e.g. meet *five* new people and learn at least *three* things about each of them.

2) How will accomplishing it impact me in a positive way?

- Think about how you can benefit from the interaction, e.g. it will make me more confident about my networking abilities.

3) How will accomplishing it impact others in a positive way?

- Think about what value you are giving to others, e.g. it will help them gain new knowledge and connections they didn't have before.

Simple, right? Remember, goals for networking should not pressure you or take away from your genuine interest in meeting people—it just gives you an opportunity to keep improving.

KNOW WHO YOU WANT TO NETWORK WITH

While networking with anyone and everyone never hurts, you should incorporate some sort of strategy to your networking approach based on your goals. For example, if you are interested in a certain job position that is available, you'll definitely want to make it a goal of yours to meet the person that's hiring, or at least who works at the company.

To decide who you want to meet, ask yourself these key questions:
1. Who can I meet that I believe seems interesting?
2. Who can I meet that is able to open up new opportunities for me and my career?
3. Who can I meet that can teach me more about things that I am passionate about and interested in?
4. Who can I meet that is currently living the dream I have in my head?

If those questions don't make you think of anyone in particular, don't worry. That just means that "anyone and everyone" is the perfect networking goal.

KNOW YOUR PITCH AND REHEARSE IT

From personal experience, we can tell you that one of the cardinal sins of networking is to go into an event unprepared to introduce yourself. We used to be very unclear about how to introduce ourselves and it caused for all sorts of anxiety and missed opportunities.

You owe it to yourself and others to know clearly how you want to introduce yourself. This not only makes you more confident while networking, but also more memorable. If others are clear on who you are and what you do, they are much more likely to be able to help you. If not right away, at least when the opportunity arises for them to help you.

The best way to find out how to introduce yourself is to combine your answers from the following questions:
1. What are you passionate about?
2. How do you want to help others? What 'pain points' do you address of others?
3. What experience do you have offering this help?
4. What challenges are you currently facing?

REVIEW A LIST OF NETWORKING QUESTIONS AND REHEARSE THEM

Having an idea of what you want to ask at a networking event can alleviate a lot of your stress before attending an event. It will not only prepare you to start conversations, but ask valuable questions that can help you make the most of other people's knowledge and wisdom. The best way to think of questions you can ask is to think of the context of the event. For example, if the event is about entrepreneurship, think of questions you can ask about entrepreneurship. What do you want to learn about entrepreneurship?

Here is a general list of questions you can use when attending a networking event:
- What made you decide to come to this event?
- What are you passionate about?
- Who have you met here today that is fascinating and why?
- What are you hoping to get from attending today?
- What is the most important thing you have learned today?
- What are some of the things you struggle with when networking? (Disarming questions can break the ice!)
- Did you meet [insert other person's name you met]?
- What are your best tips, tools or strategies for [insert topic you want to learn about]?
- How can I help you?
- How 'bout those [insert your favourite sports team name here]? :-)

WEAR APPROPRIATE ATTIRE

A lot of people dress to impress, but we would advise people to **dress to feel confident in the environment they'll be in**. For example, if wearing jeans works better for you at a conference than dress pants, go with that. However, if you feel doing so will cause you to worry you about being underdressed at the event, then it's better to dress up a bit more.

The reason we live by this principle is because people are attracted to confidence more than they are attracted to appearance. If you are comfortable in your own skin and the clothes covering it, the charisma and charm will exude from you. And who wouldn't want to look and feel their best?

Questions you can use to pick the right attire include:
- What attire represents who I am best?
- What attire makes me feel most confident and least insecure?
- What attire will alleviate any worry about how I look at the event?

Asking those questions will force you to reflect on what you're wearing in a way that will ensure you are confident in the attire.

HAVE ONE POCKET FILLED WITH BUSINESS CARDS TO GIVE AWAY, AND ONE POCKET TO COLLECT THE BUSINESS CARDS YOU RECEIVE

You'll learn later in this book that following up with people you meet is an essential skill in networking and building any relationship. While we talk more about this later, it's important that you effectively organize business cards you receive and hand out. Not only will it help you when following up, it will also add the "savvy" factor you hope to portray while networking.

The most basic way to do this is to use one pocket to store business cards you receive from others and have one pocket filled with your own business cards that you give out. This will ensure a seamless transaction when the time comes.

You might even want to create a third pocket for business cards of people you really want to build a relationship with (think of them as "first class connections") or if you don't have an extra pocket you could bend the tip of the person's card as a reminder.

The biggest thing here is to keep the business cards well organized. They are the only takeaway pieces you receive and hand out, and you don't want to have to think twice while doing it.

HAVE A WINGMAN/WINGWOMAN (if applicable)

If it's possible to bring a friend along with you to a networking event, definitely do it. Not only will it help your confidence, but it can also be a great way to join other conversations.

One thing to keep in mind for this tactic is that you must be careful you don't just speak to your friend the whole time (i.e. become cliquey or exclusive). That would just render the whole "networking" part of the event useless. Be sure you are clear on your goals and remind your friend that your reason for attending is to meet other people and expand your networks.

Here's how the wingman/wingwoman approach works:

- Simply enter a conversation together using your wingman for confidence.
- If your wingwoman is already in a conversation, they can watch for you to add you in.
- If your wing-person already had a great conversation with someone, they can introduce to their new connection.

SHOW UP WITH A SMILE

Everyone loves to see a smile. If someone isn't smiling, don't misjudge them. It may mean they're dealing with their own battles, or they are simply distracted.

Smiles are free and on-demand so be sure to come prepared to give some away!

One thing that will give you an edge is to practice your smile beforehand. As someone once wrote, "your smile is one of the most deadly weapons. So why would you not learn how to use it?"

Stand in front of a mirror and notice how you smile. Try thinking of different things in your head to see if your smile changes as well. **Once you find a smile that you like, odds are others will LOVE it!** So pay attention to what thoughts you are holding in order to achieve this perfect smile and engrain them in your memory. If you feel attractive with your smile beforehand, it will be much easier to access that same feeling in the heat of a networking event.

GET A NAMETAG

Dale Carnegie, in his popular book *"How To Win Friends and Influence People"* said that the **sweetest word to our ears is our own names**. As we grow up, most of us grow an intense emotional attachment to our names. Our names are one thing that have been there with us from the beginning without fail. We become so associated with our name, we love hearing it.

Wearing a nametag gives others the opportunity to address you by it and for you to be proud of it. Never forget that *you have a wonderful story*

and people want to hear it. So make sure you make yourself a nametag and be proud to wear it.

At most events, you should be given a nametag or the materials required to create one, so there's not much to worry about here. If you get to write your own, be sure to add your best contact method (like a website or twitter handle). If you're feeling really bold, feel free to carry your own nametag around that suits your brand.

A tip for the nametag is to wear it on the right side of your body. *Why?* Well we shake hands using our right hand so when someone goes to do it they will naturally be looking at the right side of your chest. If you're nametag is there, they'll catch it instantly.

Step 2: Starting a Conversation

CONTEXT IS KEY!

Imagine we're at a professional networking event and someone comes up to you and asks a very personal question, like "What's your religion?" There's a good chance you're going to be confused and slightly creeped out. Now it's not because that's a bad question, but the context of the event does not necessarily support that question, making it sound strange and off-putting. However, if we were at a an event about interfaith dialogue and I asked you that same question, it's perfectly valid and could probably be a great conversation starter.

No matter how you look at it, context is key. When you try to start a conversation with the right context, there's a better chance of getting a more open response and building a relationship.

While there's nothing stopping you from saying anything you want to start a conversation, it's highly advised that you think of something that is *relevant* to the person and event. For example, if you're at an entrepreneurship event, you can start a conversation by asking "Hi, so what type of business do you run?" The person will most likely **not** be taken off guard since it's a valid question in the context of the event.

TALK TO THE PERSON IN-FRONT OR BEHIND YOU AT REGISTRATION LINE

The most difficult part of networking is the beginning, especially if you show up to an event where you do not know anyone. The first opportunity that you will probably have to meet people is in the registration line. There are people in front of you and behind you silently waiting to get into the event. It's a perfect opportunity to turn to the person in front of you or behind you to strike up a conversation. Remember that the context is there–you're there to meet people and so are they—and **context is the best catalyst for connection.**

The best way to begin this type of conversation is to think of something that is very relevant to the other person in that moment. For example, you could ask, "Are you excited for the event?" or "Have you been to this event before?"

APPROACH THE ORGANIZERS

One of the best points of contact at an event are the organizers. Why? Well, there's good chance they know a lot of people in attendance and they can connect you. Now sometimes the organizers can be really busy and hard to locate, but if you manage to meet them, don't miss the opportunity to build the relationship and get connected with people they know.

If you don't know who the organizers are, ask around. If you find them, you'll want to build the relationship with them by getting to know them. Once you feel like you've shared enough info with each other, be sure to ask them if they can connect you with others they know. What's great about this is that they already have built trust with their contacts and so you can leverage that trust in order to meet some new people. Remember that the hosts probably won't connect you unless you ask (their minds are probably worried about a million other things), so don't be afraid to ask them to introduce you to others.

APPROACH PEOPLE AT THE FOOD/DRINK TABLE

Most events have a section at events for refreshments. You'll notice that when you go there to grab something to sip or munch on, it's a very silent affair. This is a great opportunity for you to strike up a conversation with other people that are there!

What's great is you even have something easy to start talking about. "Wow, look at all the food! What do you recommend?" or "Have you tried the coffee?" The reason these lines work so well is because they're related to the current focus of the other person that's there—the food and drinks!

APPROACH SOMEBODY WHO IS ALONE - OR - GROUPS OF 3

While there's no hard and fast rule about who you approach at a networking event, there are some "easier" conversation entry points you can look for.

When someone is standing alone, they're obviously the easiest person to approach. The most likely reason they are alone is because they unsure of how to network effectively. [Why not tell them about this book 😊] For this reason, there's a high likelihood that they will be even more excited to speak with you. Take advantage of the perfect opportunity and go up to them to simply say, "Hi, how are you?"

The next best entry is into a group of three. The reason for this is that we often feel most comfortable talking one on one. But when there's three, someone usually feels a bit left out. By joining that group of three, you now create the opportunity to form two pairs of people talking. It's a natural separation that won't make anyone feel awkward or unwelcomed.

ASK FOR A NEW INTRODUCTION FROM ANYONE YOU MEET OR ALREADY KNOW

If you attend an event and happen to meet someone you know, it's a great time to briefly catch up and then see if there are any new connections you can make based on relationships they have already formed.

An easy way to do this is to ask them if they know anyone else at the event. If they say yes, just express interest that you'd love to meet them. It's a "warm lead" with others where a certain level of trust already exists based on your relationship with their friend.

USE YOUR ENVIRONMENT TO THINK OF THE FIRST QUESTION

Coming up with an opening question can be one of the toughest parts of networking. "What should I ask first?" is a common networking question people have. A great lesson we learned from someone while travelling is to use your environment to come up with questions. The environment is ever-changing and easy to reference, so leveraging it for the sake of conversation makes complete sense. Just think of all those stories you hear of a person who enters the office of a CEO and strikes up a conversation about something they see in the office, like a statue or an award. All of a sudden, the conversation takes a light-hearted turn and both parties are enjoying each other's company. After rapport is built, there is room for an honest conversation about opportunities.

In the same way, you'll need to start practicing how to do this at events. Whether it's the theme of the event, the speakers you just heard, or the venue's decoration, use whatever is around you as a way to get a conversation going.

The best part about this tactic is that the environment ALWAYS has something you can use. If you think it doesn't contain something to talk about, you're not looking hard enough.

USE A CLEAR AND CONCISE INTRODUCTION

The last thing you want to do while at the event is to be thinking about how you're going to introduce yourself. Doing so only causes you to get "stuck in your head" and miss out on important information others or the environment are providing you. So we encourage you to plan how you want to introduce yourself in advance. Practice in front of a mirror or with your roommate until you are comfortable about how you express who you are and what you do. Don't forget the importance of eye contact and a handshake. Once it's committed to memory and practiced, you won't have to worry about it while actually networking. You will notice the benefits immediately as your mind will be clear to listen effectively to other people without concern to what you're going to say next.

The basic points you want to get across in your introduction is:

- Your name (if you have a tough name to pronounce do it clearly and slowly)
- What you do
- Why you do it
- Where you're going

Obviously, you can expand on these points as much as you want depending on the context and time constraints of the conversation you're in. The biggest thing you want to do is to ensure you properly express what you do so that the person listening to you will think of you if the right opportunity arises.

Step 3: Carrying a Conversation

USE OPEN-ENDED QUESTIONS

The main objective in any networking situation is to **create conversation that leads to connection**. If you ask questions that only require a "yes" or "no" answer—you've failed. OK, that's a bit harsh, but using open ended questions allows you to get a proper response from someone. And this will give you more information to carry on a conversation, gather valuable information and build the relationship.

Great open-ended questions can go like this:

- So tell me what you think of this event? (vs. "Do you like this event?")
- What was your favourite place to travel to and why? (vs. "Do you like to travel?")

KNOW THE BEATS OF A CONVERSATION

Imagine you were in a math class and then all of a sudden the teacher starts reciting English poetry. You would be confused, right?

In the same way, ensure that you are aware of the beats in a conversation. If you are talking about one thing, be careful not to shift topics suddenly. Keep learning about the topic in discussion until you can naturally move on to another topic.

LOOK FOR COMMONALITIES (INTERESTS, EXPERIENCES, CHALLENGES, ETC.)

People love talking about what they love—their kids, their hobbies, their favourite artist, etc. Try to find something you both love and chat about it. Doing this will keep you and the other person naturally interested in the conversation.

After you've built a trusting rapport with someone, feel free to find other common things to talk about that might not be things you love, such as your struggles and challenges. If you can get to this point, we promise you will find a deeper connection with someone else. When people share struggles, they are dropping their guard to you since they no longer feel vulnerable to being judged. So the earlier you can identify a common struggle between you and the other person, the sooner you can get to that deeper place. Acknowledge and honour their struggles before continuing to share your own.

STAY CURIOUS

People love to talk about themselves, so imagine if you are curious to learn more about them! It's a rare skill that they will pick up on and appreciate immediately. The more curious you can be while networking, the less you'll worry about yourself (how you look, act, or are being judged) and the more you'll be excited to talk to other people.

The best way to build your curiosity is to find something about the other person you want to learn about and ask them questions about it. If you're struggling to find that "thing", challenge yourself to become curious about something you may not be interested in mainly because you don't know enough about it.

TELL STORIES

You've read the book yet you still went to see the movie. Why's that? You knew the ending already, but it was never about that. You enjoyed the story and wanted to experience it in a different way.

Our minds naturally gravitate their attention to stories, because they do an amazing job of giving us enough info to know what's going on but not all the info necessary to know what happens. Cool, eh? When listening to stories, people paint the picture of what you're telling them in their minds as though they are experiencing it themselves with you. This visualization is a powerful way to connect with people and engage their attention.

We could write a whole book on stories, and maybe we will someday, but long story short, just talk as though you're describing an epic movie scene. Take the listener from where everything started to where it finally ends.

ASK FOR STORIES

No one likes to talk to someone who does all the talking. Listening takes up a lot of energy and talking is a way to release that energy so there's a proper energy exchange in a conversation. Besides, a person doing all the talking is really just talking to themselves and not really having a conversation with another person at all.

For that reason, don't be afraid to ask people you're talking to to tell you stories. If they say something interesting, ask them to tell you more or to give you a scenario of when they experienced what they told you. We usually ask people for their story during a coffee meeting and it's funny to see them hesitate because they don't know where to begin. However, once they get into it they love it and will share a lot of cool things that will allow you to get to know them better.

AVOID TOUCHY SUBJECTS

We all have different beliefs about certain things. Sometimes those beliefs can evoke a lot of emotion and discussing different perspectives can be very difficult to do calmly. For that reason, it's best to avoid subjects that may lead to arguing or anger. We're not saying to never talk about those things, but a networking event is probably not the best place. You've just met the person and the trust between you is low. Once you build the relationship, and the trust, your conversations will become a safer place to discuss sensitive topics.

RESPECT OTHERS BELIEFS

If you don't agree with someone else, be careful not to label them "wrong". People feel their beliefs are truths, as well as a piece of their personal identity. Just because you might see things from a different perspective, doesn't mean it's wise to shut down the conversation by attacking their beliefs. If you can really come to grasp that you can respect and connect with a person who holds different beliefs, you will not only gain more power in networking but in life in general. You will have an easier time relating to people and less time letting your ego interfere with your success.

THINK OF CONNECTIONS FOR THE OTHER PERSON

They often say you have to give to get. And it couldn't be more true. That's how our economy works! If you want to buy something you need to give money first.

The easiest thing you can give someone in the world of networking is connections with other people that might be able to help them. It might be a friend of yours who can given them advice about an experience they're about to undergo or a person that might be able to offer them services they're looking for.

There are so many things you can give, but often people don't look for them because they're too busy looking for what they can get. So next time you're at an event, focus on giving to those you meet as much as you can and watch what happens!

CLEARLY SAY WHAT YOU 'LIKED' ABOUT SOMETHING THE OTHER PERSON SAID

When you don't like the service at a store, you may be quick to vent to the manager or rant about it on Facebook. But how often do you acknowledge people for the good things they do?

People love to know when they're doing well or what you like about them. It's makes the person feel like they matter—and they'll remember you for it. Just think about when your parents said they're proud of you or your friends told you they think you're awesome. We all love those warm, fuzzy moments!

Be sure to give those same moments to others. Pick out what you like about them (genuinely) and tell them!

INVITE OTHER PEOPLE INTO THE CONVERSATION (IF APPLICABLE)

If you notice other people outside of a conversation, try your best to invite them into yours. Not only does this make them feel like they matter, but it also allows you to meet more people at once. Now you won't have to start a whole new conversation with them after the one you had, but instead you can have those two separate conversations simultaneously. At a networking event, this is great because you usually don't have a lot of time to connect. So meeting more people in a shorter amount of time always helps, as long as you take the time to properly connect.

GO INTO DEEP CONVERSATIONS ONLY IF IT MAKES SENSE

Every once in awhile, you will find yourself getting into a conversation that goes a little deeper. In most cases, this can be an incredibly rewarding and connective experience. This might happen when you ask a random question to somebody and the answer they give you contains enough raw honesty to take the conversation to a new level. If it makes sense and you are willing, you can and should engage with them.

Make sure you give gratitude for being open with you. When someone has the courage to share more open honesty or vulnerability, it is a wonderful chance to reciprocate the best you can in order to create a more powerful connection. Try to share something relevant of equivalent depth and length. However, deeper conversations have to be something that all parties are ready for. If you are not comfortable, you can exit the conversation using the techniques in the next chapter.

FIND OPPORTUNITIES TO LAUGH AND SMILE - KEEP IT FUN!

Maya Angelou said it best, *"People may forget what you did, people may forget what you said, but they will never forget how you make them feel."* Laughing and smiling always make people feel good (as long as you're not laughing at them of course!) and that feeling is something they will always relate to you in the future. When they think of you, they will remember what a great time I had with you. So keep things fun and remember that even though you might not leave with any tangible outcomes from the conversations you have, that feeling you left with the other person will come back to you tenfold.

IF APPROPRIATE, PHYSICAL CONTACT IS HELPFUL FOR DEEPER CONNECTION

If you ever watch a video of Bill Clinton meeting a dignitary while he was in presidency, you will almost always notice him touching the arm of the other person in a subtle and gentle way. Bill was a master of human relations. He knew the small things that made a big difference and that physical touch was one of them.

Now, like any tactic you employ, you need to use discretion and be clear on your intention. If you don't feel confident in yourself or your networking abilities, you might not want to try this step yet. However, as you gain practice, you'll be able to throw these small details in there to better connect with others and build solid relationships.

Step 4: Ending a Conversation

CONVERSATION LENGTH SHOULD BE BASED ON GOALS AND CONTEXT

Remember the goals you set up at the before heading to a networking event? You always want to keep those in mind. You also want to make sure you manage your time effectively, so you can accomplish all your goals. If you don't have many goals and your intention is just to build new relationships, don't worry too much about the length of your conversations. On the other hand, if you have specific objectives for the event, you'll want to be sure you keep your conversations short yet meaningful so you stay on track.

INTERRUPT THE OTHER PERSON POLITELY IF THERE IS NO NATURAL BREAK

If you want to get out of a conversation and you feel that it's not coming to a natural close, you might need to interrupt the other person.

It works best to politely say, "I'm so sorry to interrupt, but _____" with the blank being your reason why you wish to close conversation. You can also reassure the person that you'll connect with them after to keep building the relationship.

EXCUSE YOURSELF IF YOU ARE IN A GROUP SETTING

If you need to leave a conversation with a group of people, be sure to politely excuse yourself. In this case, it may not be necessary to explain why you're leaving since no one is being left alone. However, if you feel that your exit could be misinterpreted, feel free just to share a quick reason as to why you are leaving and look around the circle to give smiles and eye contact before leaving.

EXPRESS GRATITUDE FOR A CONVERSATION

Anyone you talk to is investing their time and energy in you. You should always show gratitude for that. Even if you feel that you helped them more than they did to you, keep in mind that their mere presence is helping you learn something about yourself that you aren't aware of yet.

EXCHANGE CARDS (OR CONNECT ON SOCIAL MEDIA)

The best way to exchange cards is to ***ask for theirs first***. The reason for this is because when you ask for someone's card, it is showing you are interested in them. When you give your card first, it can come across more like you want them to be interested in you and you don't care about them. This will make your exchange seem less mutual and they will appreciate it less. In addition, asking for the other person's card allows you to follow up with them as we'll discuss in the next stage. You can also ask to connect on social media. Keep in mind that asking to connect on a networking site like LinkedIn or a public conversation like Twitter is more appropriate than a site like Facebook that's mostly used with good friends and family.

TAKE A SELFIE (IF APPROPRIATE) TO DOCUMENT AND SHARE THE EXPERIENCE

If you feel you've built a good relationship with the person you met, you might want to invite them to take a selfie with you. This may seem silly, but it's a great way to end the conversation on a fun and memorable note. It's also a great excuse to reach out to them, because you can offer to send it to them.

OFFER A HANDSHAKE OR HUG

When you are finished a conversation, we highly recommend you end with a handshake. It is a sign of appreciation to the other person for giving you their time and energy. It also acts as an "official" ending to your current conversation. Occasionally, if the conversation ventures into more personal territory, a hug can be a powerful thing. But only initiate a hug if you're certain it would be positively received.

LOOK FOR ANYONE YOU PRE-TARGETED FOR A CONVERSATION

There might be events you attend where you want to speak to someone specific. It's important to try to meet them as soon as possible, so you don't miss out on your opportunity. If you are in another conversation, but you notice you have a chance to speak to the person you targeted ahead of time, just be honest with the person you're talking to and explain to them you set a goal to meet the other person and why you did.

Most people won't be offended by your early departure. The key is to communicate why you are doing so.

Stage 5: Following Up

MAKE SURE YOU FOLLOW UP WITHIN 48 HOURS!

Many people don't send follow-up emails after a networking event. This is probably the biggest mistake you can make. Any business card you get is a relationship which can lead to opportunities down the road. By not following up, you've basically turn that valuable lead into just another piece of cardboard to clutter your desk.

An easy way to make this follow up is to:

1. Place the stack of cards in front of you.
2. Write each person a personalized email that expresses your gratitude for meeting them. Be sure to also include anything they said/did that stood out to you.
3. Save their contact info and add a note that reminds you of who they are, what they do, and where you met.

Create a clear message, including gratitude for the connection and any relevant hopes or goals you have for the connection. If possible, offer some sort of value when first following up. Remember, offering your help will distinguish you from most other people. People love when thoughtful help is offered, so be sure to think of anything that might be helpful to your contact based on your conversation at the event and add it to your follow up email. It could be a link to an article, a connection with someone else, a book they should check out, or maybe just advice you have that you didn't share in person.

What you'll notice is that the more you give, the more you'll get. Now you might not get something from that same person, but the practice of helping others will eventually lead to big things from some of your contacts. Help others and others will help you. It's as simple as that.

One caution here is to not give anything just for the sake of giving. Don't just throw info at someone that is not relevant to them and won't be appreciated. Really try to pick things that can help them with a challenge they shared with you in conversation. If they've mentioned it as a challenge, it means they're looking to solve it.

ORGANIZE YOUR CONTACTS

Before the days of social media, we would organize all of our contacts in an Excel sheet or an email group. Now you can still do this with your smartphone contacts, social networking lists and even business cards. Keep track of how you know them and sort them into different groups—university, family, co-workers, Conference "X", etc. This organizing time, although only a few seconds per contact, can be a huge advantage when sending a message or sharing connections later on.

MAINTAIN TRUST WITH CONTACTS BY CONTINUING TO OFFER VALUE

Whenever you meet someone or see an opportunity that might be valuable to a person in your network, connect with them. This shows that you are thinking of them and may cause them to think of you when a relevant opportunity arises. People appreciate that you think of them and if your focus is to add value for them, you will get more in return from those that do care even if some do not.

ALWAYS REMAIN TRUE TO YOU

The term "fake it till you make it" goes against the principles of authentic networking and creating true connections with people. It is something all people use and believe to some degree, for example, when we are especially "on" at a job interview. In the end, you want real relationships that are based on honesty and integrity.

IF YOU DON'T HEAR FROM A CONTACT AFTER A WEEK, DO A SECOND FOLLOW-UP

If you really want a reply from someone, don't be afraid to follow up for a second time.

Don't assume they did not reply to your initial follow-up because they don't want to connect with you. Sometimes people get busy, sometimes they lose track of emails or sometimes they just don't realize you were expecting a reply.

Approach your second follow up as though you're just reaching out again and be clear on what you're asking for. If you don't receive a reply after a second follow-up though, it's time to give that person some space. If they contact you at a later date, great! Continue to be friendly and positive with them to honour their effort and get the most from the connection.

KEEP COMMUNICATING

If you feel a relationship is worth investing in, keep the communication with them going. Something we always say in our speaking engagements is, "You gotta want it!" Do you want to get noticed? Do you want to make an impact? Do you want your networking to lead to something valuable? Those who make a consistent, positive effort to connect get noticed.

The best way to know if it investing in a relationship is worth it or not is how much of a "win/win" it is. Take the time to evaluate how beneficial the relationship is to you and how valuable the relationship to them. If both of you are benefiting significantly from the relationship, keep nurturing it so that those benefits continue.

CONCLUSION

If you attend a live event, particularly one with a strong networking focus, you are going to a place filled with people who want to meet you! The context is set for you to introduce yourself. Firmly plant this in your head if you ever feel nervous or hesitant. People expect you to be networking and they are hoping to connect as well.

Using the techniques and tools we have given will give you a noticeable edge over everyone else. **Commit to showcasing your value, offering your support to others and building the relationship in an authentic way.** When you make people feel great, they will also think greatly of you, which ultimately leads to greater connections and opportunities.

NEXT UP

After you've practiced your networking skills in person, be sure to keep an eye out for our next book which is designed to help you network on social media! You'll learn tools and tactics that work in the online world and allow you to build great relationships from the comfort of your laptop.

First though, you need to build your confidence in live event networking. It's vital to your overall networking success. So keep practicing and applying what we've taught you and we can't wait to see the life-changing effects it has.

Be sure to let us know about your live event networking experiences by emailing us at raehanbobby@gmail.com and im@ryancoelho.com.

(Yes, these are our real and personal e-mail addresses!)

WHO WE ARE

Bobby Umar

Bobby is a 4-time TEDx speaker, internationally published author, Huffington Post contributor and Leadership catalyst.

A champion of authentic connection, 'lost leaders' and heart-based leadership, Bobby brings an engaging presence, endless exuberance and dynamic people skills to his presentations. With a background in brand marketing, engineering and the performing arts, Bobby draws on his diverse 20-year career to lead Raeallan, whose mission is to discover, inspire and develop leadership in Gen Y and Gen X.

Thousands of people across North America have felt a deep connection with Bobby's energetic keynotes and funny personal stories on personal branding, networking and social media. With over 250,000 followers on social media, he has been ranked the 4th biggest leadership influencer on social media and the 2nd best business coach to follow on Twitter.

Learn more at http://raeallan.com

Ryan Coelho

With a passion for personal development and love of people, Ryan Coelho has dedicated the past few years of his life developing others and energizing audiences.

He focuses on bringing a high energy approach to his presentations in order to get people excited about bettering themselves; learning to get what they want in life; and most importantly, finding out how to get out of their own to do so.

Some key highlights of Ryan's career include speaking at TEDxRichmondHill; receiving a standing ovation from 1000 students at Queen's University; and producing his popular program personal development, Engineering Success.

Learn more at http://RyanCoelho.com

Made in the USA
Charleston, SC
06 October 2014